FREE VERSE EDITIONS

EDITED BY JON THOMPSON

Also by Jennifer Atkinson

Canticle of the Night Path

Drift Ice

The Drowned City

The Dogwood Tree

THE THINKING EYE

Jennifer Atkinson

Parlor Press
Anderson, South Carolina
www.parlorpress.com

Parlor Press LLC, Anderson, South Carolina, 29621

Printed in the United States of America
S A N: 2 5 4 - 8 8 7 9

Library of Congress Cataloging-in-Publication Data

Names: Atkinson, Jennifer, 1955- author.
Title: The thinking eye / Jennifer Atkinson.
Description: Anderson, South Carolina : Parlor Press, [2016] | Series: Free Verse Editions
Identifiers: LCCN 2015044951 (print) | LCCN 2015048127 (ebook) | ISBN 9781602357884 (softcover : acid-free paper) | ISBN 9781602357891 (pdf) | ISBN 9781602357907 (epub) | ISBN 9781602357914 (ibook) | ISBN 9781602357921 (Kindle)
Classification: LCC PS3551.T57 A6 2016 (print) | LCC PS3551.T57 (ebook) | DDC 811/.54--dc23
LC record available at http://lccn.loc.gov/2015044951

Printed on acid-free paper.

Parlor Press, LLC is an independent publisher of scholarly and trade titles in print and multimedia formats. This book is available in paperback and ebook formats from Parlor Press on the World Wide Web at http://www.parlorpress.com or through online and brick-and-mortar bookstores. For submission information or to find out about Parlor Press publications, write to Parlor Press, 3015 Brackenberry Drive, Anderson, South Carolina, 29621, or email editor@parlorpress.com.

Contents

for Clare and Rob

THE THINKING EYE

Art does not reproduce the visible but makes visible.

—*Paul Klee*

We will save only what we love and we will love only what we know.

— *Baba Dioum*

At the Chernobyl Power Plant Eco-Reserve

If ravens perch on the ferris wheel
outside of town, if owls
nest in the silos and swallows circle
the tipped watchtower, if catfish
bloat in the cooling pool and elk
graze on perennial beard grass,
if boars rake their tusks
among the roots, if black
storks claim the cloud-blighted
pines of Red Forest, if wire
succumbs to rust, if lichen,
if shingles unhinge in the snow,
if untrafficked lots cede land
to yarrow, if mirrors, if spoons
reflect the sky, if watches tick
in unopened drawers, if swollen,
if stiff-maned Przewalsi horses
foal, if wolves, if then, if then, if

ONE

Landscape of One Hundred Words

Of stone, fern, blood, and water I mumble,
trying out phrases, sounds

as distinct as the teasel's shadow,
gestures of mind and music,

as gnawed at and off-plumb
as a mushroom's gilled undercap,

as easily smoothed away
as a water strider's V-ed wake,

useless as a junco's dissevered
wing, less aware than a sleeping owl,

twice as invasive as loosestrife,
half as responsive as touch-me-not.

Quartz is far more consoling and true.
Words are not the silver sage

of olive leaves, the untethered milkweed
drift of down, but paltry things,

leaf-litter through which push up
foamflowers, black snakes, shrews and turbans.

The Laws of Succession

Asters to ashes, dogwood to liriodendron: wild has its way.

The afterlife is the understory—maple samaras in a red whirl,
a downdraft over a deadfall; out of cold dormancy too early,

it seems to me, but what do I know?

Turkeys, a nodding flock of twelve at least,
a quorum, a jury, trample the duff of twenty years

ago when highbush blue- and lowbush huckleberry

held this ridge with birch and bobwhite quail,
and one little pin oak with its shadow of ground pine.

Now a copse of young silver beeches, their last year's

leaves chattered cold in the wind, has shaded out the bushes,
overbrowsed anyhow by too many white-tailed deer,

barely skittish, willing just yards from the house

to graze the back lawn, itself returned, reversing
the laws of succession to bitten down grasses, to pasture.

The Seven Stars of the Little Dipper

1.

how to in patience

untangle
from the weft

of root-hairs furred
in dust and the gloss

of mycorrhiza—
their spreading threads

a nervous
inter-order—

I?

2.

one word
an exhalation

caught in the syntax
of weather

vapor spore smoke pollen
wind off the high plains

breathed
through lungs gills stomata

or trapped
a thousand years in glacial ice

to fizz on the tongue
when a chipped shard melts

3.

a child squats in the straw

sings to ease
her goat her voice
the clean fragrance of milk

4.

if in that language too
is almost a homonym of *yes*

5.

bleared in the night
stars twin stars a solar system

space flattened—like earth
mercatored—to sky

light-year-long gaps
are thumbs' breadths of black

darkness dipped from darkness
that cold that good

6.

how to
frac

from the shale
silt

from the silt
green

to lift
from enstonement

memory a fern
lithe beside the pool

7.

Cool from the spring—

she remembers the cup
there on the rock

you dipped and drank

I dipped and drank

Landscape with Goat's Eye

A page where the flip-book of memories
Always opens
                                    or when thumbed through
Stutters and stops:

The road is a pale dust track.
The bullock's hoofbeats muffled,
                                                                        wooden
Cartwheels creak.
                                        On the horizon
The high fig tree, fruitless in this season,
Rocks with the jounce of the cart.

Through sleepy Bodh Gaya, a boy
Rides his slope-shouldered buffalo
Past temples and tea stalls, pilgrims and tourists.
Among them but refusing,
                                                  stubborn,
The tree's sacred shade
I buy bread and bananas and feed
The peels and overripe bits to the goats.

The dust is a variorum of tracks. The bullock's
Hooves beat steady, wooden

Cartwheels creak.
                                       On the horizon and overhead
The pale, changeable, cataracted sky.

I set sweet rice aside on the plate
                                                                        practicing
Renunciation, practicing restraint
(Or was it compassion?)
                                              and the goats

Butt and nudge, more than companionably.

So much forgotten, but not
That goaty, cowlicked, knobby head,
                                        the loose drape of her ears,
And that fixed eye, a sliver
Of goat-inscrutable gold leaf
                                as if lifted
From an icon sky,
                      barely lustrous, sheer, and creased.

The road from the station is pale.
The bullock's hoofbeats, weathered
                                      traces, wooden
Cartwheels creak,
Wearing furrows in the dust.

Drawn from Memory

Jacaranda flowers fall,
hundreds of petals
                                        among a few coins.
When the sleeping man wakes
and hoists himself up from the Kathmandu pavement,

he'll leave his shadow behind on the square.

𝄽

A thousand lit
                                distinct moments, caught
each one like a raindrop on a thorn,

a thorn on a briar bent over
a river high on snow melt and April—
all around the unfurling of leaves.

𝄽

Half this, half that. Tadpoles quick in the pond.
Oak catkins fat and dusting down pollen.

He tore off his sister's shirt. "See?"
How not to look?
                                        Her shame. Her fury.
Nancy, the first of us girls to grow breasts.

𝄽

The historical Buddha is said to have said, if not in so many words, that moonlight falls as brightly on the sea as the river, the puddle, the rain-filled divot a deer leaves in the dirt. In this time, a buddha would surely add the galvanized metal trashcan lid or the refugee's blue plastic tent. But what does it *mean?* we want to ask. What is the moon in that metaphor? What is the blazing sun?

⁂

Why remember this and not that?
A stranger's cool glance and not my grandfather's eyes filled with tears.
Further in summer than the birds or *rough in the distant glitter* but not
What he said when he woke without his name.

What are we that we spend our hours
hoarding and end with empty hands?

⁂

A subway car
jammed with bodies, none talking,
all seething with plans and complaints,
after-work weariness, longing,
or sly pleasure in contact?

So many of us, each sealed in a separate skin.

⁂

Alone once in the woods, I slipped off a cliff, slammed down among boulders, rolled another twenty feet, and fetched up against the side of a moldering deadfall. At least that's where I woke, dizzy and more-or-less unhurt. This is you, I thought, feeling lucky, not just because I'd survived the fall but because I still held in my hand, uncrushed, a tiny blue half egg shell, still damp inside, and with a wisp, an eyelash, of feather stuck to the orange smear.

⁂

Ink-brushed plum blossom and bristly pine:

Winter's shadow cast on the walls.
Outside in the tok-tok of wood clogs,
teahouses spread their cloths.

Red rice-paper parasols bob and twirl,
toys in the dizzying snow.

Switchbacking, hot, down out of the mountains,
a slate-roofed village on the slate path.
An up-gust. Chill. Hail-clatter and -sting.
Ice then like realized joy.

All of it gone now, returned to rubble in the earthquake.

Hailstones that melt on the tongue, a little salty,
lift like steam, as steam,
from the path.

Landscape with Jeffers and the Connecticut River

Oat stalks hang their oat-heavy heads.
Panic grass shakes in the wind
off a goldfinch's wing. Cause,
effect, and cause.

Drone, like the bee, of goldenrod and aster,
tool of the stick-tight and cockleburr,
I park and wade into high riverside grasses.

A dog gnaws on a box turtle, a spider rides
a floating log, straining the air of its midges and leafbits.
A fisherman lazy as late summer current,
casts, reels, and casts.

It occurs to me I am alive, which is to say
I won't be soon. Robinson Jeffers
from Carmel Point, in "an unbroken field of poppy and lupin"

ashamed of us all (of himself), took solace in time,
in salt, water, and rock, in knowing
all things human "will ebb, and all/
Their works dissolve."

Me, too. And I'm not always so patient. I've caught myself
wishing our spoiler species gone, just swept away,
returned to rust and compost for more deserving earthly forms.

Meanwhile, flint arrowheads turn up among the plastic
picnic sporks, the glacial crags and bottom silt.
Hawks roost across the river on the now defunct
nuclear power plant cooling tower,

flotsam left at the human high water mark.
Like mussel shells, like driftwood or seedpod,
like the current's corrugations in the sand.

Here, on this side, a woodchuck sits up, lustrous,
fat on her chestnut haunches, (she thinks herself
queen of her narrow realm) and munches
the fisherman's crust.

Who wouldn't smile? Who doesn't pity—and love—
the woodchuck not only despite but *for* her like-human smugness?
How can I not through her intercession forgive
for now a few things human.

Landscape with Peregrine Falcon and Hart Crane

Tilting there momently on the girder, wings closed, alert
to wind shifts, unfazed by the river below, the clang, the constant
trafficking back and forth, a falcon waits on the side rail.
Sunlight sheers off low through the cables;
exhaust like coal-dust blackens the green bolted steel.
The lower level is pitched into echo-y dark, head- and taillights
flash among the beams; the upper level's trucks whine.
No harp or altar, the GW trembles and sways.

The far bank rusts through the haze; barges shed froth.
The peregrine swivels her head, her icy gaze, waits,
musters her fury and vaults
into space to seize a slow-wheeling pigeon.
Ahead across the Hudson, a string of shiny cars
threads the EZ-Pass lanes to New England.

The Thinking Eye

after Paul Klee

The green eye of the forest opens
and its twin, the moon, appears—lidless,
unshuttable, the afterimage of fire.

It's getting dark. It's getting late in the season.
The deer stiffen to hieroglyphs, the mountains
fade and blear. The trees, for the moment

unsusceptible to wind, are impassive.
That's how it is after a war.
Stuccoed pillars left half-built, tiny

figures of refugees, hands up in surrender
or perhaps farewell, *goodbye, goodbye.* A little eagle
not flying, its underwings show white.

Landscape with Palm and Irises

Assisi, Italy

It's Spring again, not quite Easter,
and right on time, the pear trees
froth, the wood thrush sings,

and irises fatten on swaying stalks,
their sword-shaped leaves fanned out
like the palm in Giotto's "Flight into Egypt."

His single palm tree bends to shield,
or as if to shield, one swaddled child.
Over the child and parents hangs a moonless sky.

The iris flowers when they bloom
here next week will spill a blue as blue
as the frescoed mother's dress; the sun will unseal

the calyxed buds, a force and result
as predictable as malice. And yet
for Giotto's escaping family, nothing blooms. Nothing

promises to flower either. Or fruit. Not even
the Flight scene's usual trope, those lucky
grapes or dates. No distractions, no not knowing

what they are running from. No wind
snuffs or muffles the cries, the hooves,
the sword-clang noise from the next fresco panel:

the Slaughter of the Innocents.
It and the Flight are side-by-side.
Knowing burns and burns

under her cloak, a nightmare
she can't soothe, can't wake
or run from, no matter how hard he tugs the donkey's rope,

how close the angels hover,
how late she sits up watching
the baby sleep, she can't rest. Neither can she

regret escaping, even knowing
others' sons are dying while—because—
she saved her own and left so many others unwarned.

Does she really believe they've eluded
the emperor's sword? Like clockwork
the story turns and turns, spring by spring, until

with the blooming iris, the horror
comes around again to claim
their naked child. To everything its season.

Self-Portrait with Sequoia Semper Virens

Under and among them, their straight-up trunks,
        some hollow, some charred in a long ago fire—
their crowns a world away, two hundred feet up,

        host another separate woods,
where ferns sprout in pockets of wind-gathered dirt,
        huckleberries bloom and set fruit,

rain ponds in clefts and burls, and—.
        Here on the ground, I tend to reverie.
The fog's not blown or burnt off yet.

        In light wind a handful of dewdrops shakes loose,
loud on the leaves of the understory.
        Downslope, creek noise and the knife-on-whetstone

cry of a jay honing *awake, awake* to new keenness.
        Hard advice. I'm drawn
to the hollow dark inside the trees,

        as if I might inhabit sequoia time and willing
pliancy, as if the moss light,
        the fire-blackened caves in the trees

might quell my fidgets and pesky ideas,
        slow my heart and lungs so I might unselve awhile.
Nature, whatever it is, isn't a book

of lessons—a revelation on every page—
        but who hasn't seen patterns in the symmetries
and randomness? Only non-pattern-seeking species.

        Who hasn't coveted the deer's agility
or hearing the chickadee's call not wished to answer?
        The tree's hollow extends farther than I can see.

Reaching up, I stir a soundless flutter of moths
            (soundless at least to human ears)
and brush loose a cobweb. Not that it matters.

            By morning, the torn web will be restrung,
not quite as before
            but close enough for spiders and moths.

Landscape with Translucent Moon

Palm trees, like old pilings, tip
in the sand toward the Maldive Islands still.
The moon,
                    a slice of green coconut, floats
in a sky streaky with cloud.

Ten winters after the tsunami hit,
                                        off-shore
the coral reef is reinventing itself
by fits and starts, by hook and foot
and reef-wasn't-built-in-a-day
                                    steady calm.
Patience comes easy to gastropods.

The after-war
news is of atrocity, in this like
                                    before-, during, after-
war news everywhere: rape, torture, mass graves,
the usual list, human power
reasserting itself
                        on the bodies of others.

Deep in the once
                        jungled, once war-riven
Tamil north, a Buddha carved in living stone
still falls smiling into death,
                                    serene these last thousand years.
How many wars
has that peace survived?

It's said that just before he died,
the historical Buddha
                            sent south to Sri Lanka
a slip from the original
enlightenment tree at Bodh Gaya.

That tree planted between the sites of tsunami and war
is now the oldest tree on earth, a living
                                        emblem of compassion
for these last two thousand years.
It's guarded night and day at gunpoint.

TWO

Reading By Riverlight

Fluster and scuff, upwell and downshift, all motion the Gihon surface
crimps, crams, rucks, and scars—on the skids, at a slant, on the sly.

Alongside a tangle at silt-edge of jetsam, a water-built scree
of this, that, and the other, quick or decaying, resisting the drag downstream.

West out of Eden, the river's a clean slate, erased and erasing,
doodled on, scratched at, chalked up with practice strokes and aimless

curlicues in readiness for what comes, nothing or—no—
nothing *and* floodwash (snowmelt, downpour) the onrush of visible things.

𝄽

She called it "The Nostalgia of the River Gihon," her green encaustic field,
scratched through to show the clay and sulfur underwork.

I'd have thought the river felt the reverse, the way the current
turns out its pockets, divesting itself of objects, precious and used-up alike,

offering up all it owns to its shores, renouncing all but get-on-with-it.
I mean you don't see the river turning back in regret,

or not going on about its business. What would you call it then,
she said, going over and over the same ground—rehearsal?

𝄽

Nothing needs my attention. I give it, though, anyway
in the four, the six, the ten directions, but especially through

this morning the doorframe window: eavemelt, frozen rain,
a bush strung up with vine and pods swinging a little

in a little wind. Beyond, toward the river, what I take to be
(kinked, crooked, lichened) a crabapple tree, five pines

just askant and a crow flying crosswise. As the crow flies,
the mountains are wearing away.

𝄽

The way the noise has of blurring, clash and sprayfall, drip and slosh,
to one ongoing roar, louder when you look its way or stop seeing *river*
altogether.

Notice how noticing the culvert spill foregrounds its high-pitched impact,
how calling the slide of water over what's left of the dam *lyric*

sets aside for that strain in the music, a near silence, a sound like rubbed suede.
Watch close enough the downwardness of, the dissolve

of snowfall into the largo dark and you'll hear it, the prick and unstitch
of the cold river's seams, the scatter sound of needles dropping.

𝄽

Fog moved over the face of the river, its breath on the pebbled beach
turned overnight to hoarfrost—twigs, asters, sphagnum tufts

of not-quite-snow, minute branchings and interbranchings as fine
as eyelashes, a simulacrum composed in darkness as if

of fingernail parings and strands of white hair. Far too fragile
for close inspection, one touch, one exhalation, returns—

breath for breath—the fog's creation to amorphous drops,
inseparable from the general flood of early winter.

𝄽

Tracks through first snow to the river: Which is what I can't say
—deep powder obscures all but the destination. These deep prints

nagging at my heels are evidently mine, but those I crossed
that stop at the tree might be a squirrel's or a marten's, those

spread out dents and drags could be a cottontail, running. That trail
might be fox-made or as likely a beagle's, off leash and glad to be gadding about.

A record of nothing unusual. Just the marks we make by moving—
selving and selving–one (or two) feet in front of the other(s).

❦

Before first light, she lay a plank across the thin ice—too thin by noon
to hold up a sparrow—and from that scaffold on the river erected

cattail-stalk beams, each frozen in steady. Then quickly (the sun was rising)
built a rough narthex of briar and sticks, a rush sort-of steeple and door.

The hardest part was removing the scaffold. Her chapel on the river
lasted all of half an hour before the beams listed and toppled,

the steeple and arches reverted to flotsam. I wonder, she said, how I'd feel
if I'd asked you to photograph it—even that silly frill of a steeple.

❦

If the river rose from its bed.
If the cloud sank down like a wizened balloon.

Air over the surface hums,
The resonant drone of an open string.

If the fish moon slipped from the sky.
If the flock ascended like a single bird.

Loose pollen and spores, the dust off a winter moth's wings.
A low wind so far barely breathing.

❦

Under the valley runs a marble seam; marble, old symbol of perdurance
despite its molten, morphic provenance—fossil coral and bone dust,

salts, eroded, decayed, crushed and entwined, twinned, tripleted,
pressed into lime, refired to liquid, a viscous brook flowing up

through the green flesh of what's become the Green Mountains,
themselves uptilted, thrust-faulted, glaciered over,

and rivered down to valley, this valley, where walking the snowmobile trail
out of town we kick up rocks marbled with marble like meat with fat.

Ice starts back over the shallows, a gravel bar where the river slows
to flatten the curve, the current lazy and hurried both,

easing into an oxbow, caps and recaps the stones—
gloss on gloss, a liquid to gelid history of cold

through which the midrashic river slips on underneath
to re-emerge darker downstream—creased and pleated,

infolding to fit a rapids its own motion formed,
forms, and over the rocks, works all at once to unform.

A Carolina Wren Sings on the Porch Rail

How to pin sounds to the page

with spruce gum graphite thorns
How to transpose to a singable key

to mark plosives fricatives trills and rests
to compose
an antiphon if not an answer

More shadow cast than lamplight
more brook than mirror

A live syntax
of interrogative willow
A masonry of glacial noun rubble

sgraffitoed in lichen and clay
frost- deer- and hunter-tumbled

woven over with catbriar
burrowed through
with verbs and voles

their nests lined with pinfeathers dog-hair
and the grassy susurrations of un- and de-worded vowels

Dragonflies built from dragonflies built from *dragonflies*
prism and nymph

How not to believe in
to trust for the moment the true enough

the worn-smooth weight and facets of *feldspar*
the prick and hinge
of *chinkapin husk*

the rot and savor of *under*

Almost

Only in the most resinous
woods,

the deepest of evergreen
stands would that

gloom in me
open. Solitude, inviolate

—or nearly so—
as I, could then enter.

Unlike
the laurel starved underneath for sun

I felt myself lighten,
lift

almost. The random
notes of conefall, birdsong, traffic

a quarter-mile off—
I found I was counting

breaths. Among the hemlocks
splintered

light shafts, fletched
with owl

quills, lodged
in the soft ground.

I might have
almost sung.

Wind rarely intruded.
Nor deep snow. Rain

but indirectly. Nights
the moon

hardly touched.
In a storm

deer lay up there
flank to flank, in the cold

their breath one,
I dreamed, visible cloud.

Exhalation

The O^2 and water vapor that steam
from the 9 x 9000 stomata in an oak leaf

breathe through the lungs of a squirrel,
are swept up on the draft off a hawk's wing,
caught on a breeze viscous with spores,

carried in a wood thrush call to a wood thrush
across a loosestrifed highway shoulder;

some molecules go to a meadow of factories,
their gravel lots of gleaming cars, rust-lipped silos and seagulls;
some molecules blow on over the marsh and its out-gassing roses;

further dispersing, mixing, some
rise up into a scudding cloud

and from its high scatter of vapor and ice
fall to the Rappahannock, the Hudson, the Housatonic
to fetch up 10,000,000,000 transactions later,

in a plankton bloom off Peru,
in volcanic dust over Iceland,

in the hollows of a Sendai egret's bones,
in the stinging fifty-days wind over Homs,
in the snow that falls on Chernobyl's red pines—

like as not part of the same air
that first voiced the Diamond Sutra,

or fueled the firestorm at Dresden,
that shrieks from the kitchen kettle
or a red squirrel seized by a hawk in mid-flight.

Still, Again: Thirty Years After the Assault

Gone soft in its gray socket, the late sun rots.
Snowflakes rise on a wind and refall harder,

whiter, when the gust stalls, on the witch hazel's
chafed red wands. Numbness

hits so slowly when you lie waiting, cold
and colder, the air from your mouth material

lifting away from what you once called your
self, blithely assuming

as true that self is suffused in
flesh, every cell you, not just this hovering

watchfulness, through which the snow
moves easily, unimpeded.

You are vanishing while she takes definite
shape on the brook edge, her edges

defined by what is, did, seems to be, happening, happened
in her on the freezing ground.

The Fossil Record

What if now I broke the seal—
rebroke it—
and wedged in underneath: September's

corn silk light, the river, windfall ghastly with yellow-jackets,
a fist of thistle seed,
whatever fit—not

so much to wake you as to believe for a moment
you dream the things
of my dreams. Along the river

among rounded river
stones there is a stone
on which the fossiled imprint of a leaf makes real

the imagined:
the image is its image.
Relics, bones, and splinters, hard evidence,

as if evidence were proof, is everywhere.
You are the delible
flute note, footfall, the dull clang of falling stone

against bare cliff,
outcrop,
then silence legible as distance.

What is love compared to rock?
In the story a child's hoard of pebbles
is better proof against hunger

than bread
or love. And yet
it's what doesn't

turn up from the rain-softened ground,
what doesn't
like seed from seed, return,

as the meadow, repurpled with thistles, regilded with finches, returns—
it's what it's no use
sifting the midden for I want.

Not even so much a you
who loves or responds as one who hears.
Or can seem to.

Landscape with Bloodroot

for Martha Hale Williamson : in memoriam

She demanded I pay attention,
for example, to the wildflowers we walked by,
not just the easy ones like
                                        Queen Anne's lace or butter-and-eggs,
but harder, stranger ones:
                                        trailing arbutus, hepatica, deadman's pipes.

To tell the truth I didn't always wholly love
our walks and her half-stern, half-joking catechism:
What's that?
                    What's that one called?
When she pointed to a flower I couldn't name,

we collected a sprig to bring home
to the other bible, her headstone-heavy, precious
(we had to wash our hands first)
                                                  North American Wildflowers.
She made it my work

to count the petals, assess the leaves—
serrated or smooth? lobed? alternate? waxy? downy? —
then keeping in mind the season
and context—
                        field, slope, brookside—

to page through (my favorite part) and solve the mystery.
We paired the real to the right illustration and proper name.
When I asked how a flower got its name—
                                                            Why fleabane?
cowslip? St. John's (I thought it was) Wart?

—some of the stories she knew.
                                                  Others I know now
she made up whole cloth, and at least once, stumped,
(or who knows why now?) she asked me
Why am I Martha? Why are you Jen?

She'd be saddened by how much I've forgotten—
which celandine is greater?
which blue aster is which?
and just where, in the Cockaponsett woods,
her favorite, sweet, pink-turning-white arbutus, grew.

And perhaps grows still.
I've not lost altogether, though, her lessons,
the habit of close attention,
the pleasure
of names and of seeing in the actual sprig

the guidebook's painted version,
as well as the deep,
harder here to confess
heart-leaps-up joy in recognition,
as on an April wooded hillside

when white, gold-stamened stars
open among the under-rot,
eight-petalled
from a basal rosette of bluish, lobed leaves:
(I can almost hear the name in her voice)
Bloodroot.

The Five Seeds of the Northern Spy Apple

A deer yanks an apple from the tree,
chomps, and chews up half:

the core breaks between his jaws,
and the first seed is swallowed whole.

Ruminant stomach acids
etch the seed's palisade cells

as it travels the deer's length to the ground.
Rain falls, preparing the soil.

Snow follows,
preventing the seed from sprouting too soon.

Nonetheless, in a cold March
downpour, it drowns,

rots, and reclaimed by fungi,
returns as sugar to the earth.

𝄽

The second seed cracks between the deer's teeth
and breaks down to mush in the cud.

𝄽

The third decays
among the jacked buck's offal:

stomachs and organs cut loose by flashlight and spilled
over a tumbledown roadside wall.

𝄽

Still lodged in the dropped,
uneaten half of the apple,

swarmed over with yellow-jackets,
the fourth seed molders in the fruit,

dissolving
in the hard-cider ferment of windfall.

❦

The fifth, plucked from April's
thawing heap, slides unscathed

through a turkey's craw,
lands in its nest among the detritus

of last year's eggshells, dirt, and down,
and this spring's broken, gathered sticks,

cast-off beetle wings
and acorn husks,

softening, unaccounted for, until after the nest is abandoned
and any stray feathers return to the wind.
Only then

does the last seed open, soften, and green
its apple way into the dirt.

Extinction

If we walk the marsh path up
past all but the full tide's

reach, upcreek where the water
is nearly sweet, ferns arch in

the muddy duff, and laurel,
un-salt-daunted, greens, at first

the wind feels right, dampish, just
slightly skunked, and the sun dims

like it always did. Blackbirds
screech and circling deerflies bite,

nagging as ever. Why then
this feeling, a percussive

absence, a lapse in the midst,
in spring's elsewise bright music?

It's as if a letter were
disappeared and the language

left stunted, skewed, rickety,
disabled by gaps. Can we

keep pretending the syntax
isn't shifting, isn't thin,

thinning & ?

THREE

In the Hands of the Builder

A ship wrecked off Hatteras, racked,
Swamped, foundered, and pounded under
The waves to flotsam, winds up as silver

Rubble on Greenland's graveled shore.
Half the keel, once half an oak
Felled and dragged downriver from Portland

To the Essex, Connecticut shipyard,
In the hands of the builder now becomes a roof-beam.
Planks smoothed for the ship's garstrakes

Hang now on leather hinges—a door.
And loose hunks—shards of mast
And bow-stem—burn in the stone hearth.

Copper, potassium, sodium flare
Auroras of tropic color in the white-out
Of Greenland winter—dream-fringed

Green, rose and coral mineral fire.
In the morning cold in the rubble and ash
A black ingot of ivory-hard, fire-tried

Oak for the carver to figure and pierce
Through—a knuckle-size talisman to be worn
For luck around a sailor's neck.

Local History

Outpost of fish hawk and crow, one drowned oak, one white-blooming pear—
Lodged in the craw of the hay marsh, Hag Island.

The dock pilings and john-boat long rotten, house timbers sunk in the earth,
What remains is rust, foundation stone, and a garden plot of haggard herbs.

Yarrow for bleeding, horehound for cough, catnip and boneset for fever,
Poke, foxglove, convolvulus to drive off hag-ridden dreams.

Mullein scepters, several, waist-high, faint green, each as cool
As a jar of fireflies, glow—they must have been hers—hag tapers.

Soaked in tallow, the spikes burn down to an acrid smolder
Over a feast of winnowed thistle, one black seed for each hag spirit.

Shifting winds, liens and unclear titles. Hardly an island, flotsam
Among the reeds and sedges, witch hazel, the usual haggling gulls.

Involution

The cavern is a mirror—unlit or leoparded in lantern light.

Overhung with limestone ice, its clear pool deepens one drop at a time.
The clock of years slows as it winds down.

Among the inventory of unearthed things—tallow residue, finger bone, a
toothless arc of jaw—

the dark itself is an artifact
one longs to touch the smooth, involuted as conch, contours of.

A smoke-smirched wall revealed by cell phone glow.

Manganese, rust, and ochre daubs become fish, penniped, caribou, horse—
images of their maker

as true as a stenciled hand.

Or in the calcified ash, a child's footprints
alongside the paw prints of her dog.

On Earth as It Is

Morning and morning and morning
The high-pitched tick of a cardinal
                concealed in the holly
Keeps bad time
        slows like a hand-wound left on the nightstand

Another day and another
            wood beads on a long loop
Beechnuts fallen in a beech woods
Counted or not
        burnished with handling or buried in leaf-rot

Over and over the Milosz words
"There are nothing but gifts on this poor, poor Earth"
                        Underneath
Like a line plucked on stand-up bass
                to whom to whom to whom

An archeologist working
            in the shadow of Alaska's Brooks Range
Dug into a promising hummock and found
A cache of prehistoric like-Venetian glass beads

On the dig surface equally blue in July
Jacob's ladder
        just inches tall
And a mouse-gnawed antler dissolving
                into the reindeer moss

Where 1940s nuclear testing left strontium 90
To live out its many half-lives
            one gravel truck-road
(Straight) follows the zigzagged Alyeska pipeline north

The Brooks Range flattens to
stegosaur spines
At the skyline
a scuffed-up cuttlefish bone day-moon
And beyond

A sign reading
Arctic Circle the clangor of pumps
In the town they call Deadhorse:
glassy sea and under the whiff of diesel
A diner famous for pot roast and pie

Landscape with Mud Turtle

I'd have thought by now my life would look
    half-grown, half-gone, half-something,
but I can't get far enough off to see it.
    Among the reeds, the rocking cattails,
the hollow seed pods of last summer's lilies,
    I can't for the life of me get a long view.

A doe drifts along the rise, fur fading with the season,
    stiff and lithe by turns—the same one,
I know her by the scar—I often see browsing at the edge
    where woods and marsh and graveyard lands converge.
What, I wonder, does *she* see? By what mark
    would she know me from others of my species?

When I was a girl I lay down
    in the pressed-grass hollows where the deer had slept,
and tried to dream myself a deer,
    that wordless, that meant-to-be-there.
I pressed the rough, live ends of their antlers
    against my forehead and wished.

Under the pond mud, half-frozen, dormant among the dormant,
    turtles breathe through their skins,
barely, not quite dead in their shells. Geodes.
    Come spring, come stronger light, they thaw,
gasping at ice cracks, clawing at the slush and scum,
    self-resurrected. It happens every year. Until it doesn't.

A pond turns marsh, turns meadow in no time flat:
    silting in, not drowning *all* the windblown seed that falls,
letting the alder and pussy willow take root,
    parching the pondweeds, deporting the turtles,
the snails that cling to the lily pads' undersides,
    and the waterbirds that ate them.

A transformation before your eyes.
Where I skated in spirals one winter, beech trees grow:
Silver for silver, not everything lost.
Where redwing blackbirds flew up singing
victorie, victorie, cardinals search the brambles for berries
and dogs off their leashes snuffle up rabbits.

After an icestorm, I found a wren stiff in the cold,
its russet specks and stripes magnified,
its eyes shut, its beak like something carved
and drawn on. I closed it in my hands
and, fool that I still am, blew through the gaps between my thumbs.

Landscape at 3rd Ave. and 1984

From here I can only imagine the rain
streaking the tree trunks, the creekbank weeds
soused and toppled,
                                        the creek
picking up silt and speed
on its way to the river,
                                        the river, the Mississippi, the sea
where its green and its froth will disperse in the salt.

                                        Bob's up the road
planting seeds in the downpour,
vines to climb over his thin-roofed shack—
a vision he has
                                        of leaf-light through the windows,
hollow gourd baubles tocking
                                        at the plywood walls.
Jan's halfway to work at the bookstore,
Eric's teaching *Gatsby* in Cedar Rapids.

I'm inside our first house,
                                        Eric's and mine,
with the heat turned up, my wet clothes stuffed
in the washer direct,
                                        waiting—naked, in the kitchen corner
out of the side- and picture-windows'
lines of sight—
                                        for the mailman to slog by.

Caught out of the current,
                                        snagged
a second on the thought of us all—
the blocks from Muscatine to Court,
the wider swath between rivers and highways, under rain—
each of us for the moment transfixed.
                                        Figurines in our cases
glazed against damp.

The doorknob's swollen reflections dull.
The mailbox grates on its hinges—
                                    open, shut.

One pulse beat, another, the rain.
Boots on the driveway gravel,
the mailman's cap and shoulder passing
                                    onward, onward, on-

The Understory

The sycamore doesn't lean riverward.
It leans toward the light over the river,
shading an understory beneath its green,
daunting the aster, guarding the fern,
cooling the water alongside, waters
one week raucous with parking-lot runoff,
the next nearly stagnant. Slow or quick,
the current undercuts the sycamore's bank,
leaves gravel trapped in its roots.

And the sycamore leans further, tipped
like an open drawbridge. Already

it's picked up the river's accent,
that slurred drawl, those schwa-flat vowels.
It's falling into the rhythm, accepting
the ethic of onwardness. Only we will miss
the leaning tree when it finally falls.
Its birds will choose another to light on,
deer will take its downed leaves,
asters will star in the light of its absence.
Though ferns will parch, fish will profit.

And the river will flow under,
over, forward, around its trunk, almost as before.

Oxbow River

The surface shivers and wobbles like molten
color—gray, other grays, and silvers—

folded, it seems, back on itself. Afloat
on the river, who doesn't think of time?

Over gray and other grays, silver
reflections warp and blur

on the river. Who doesn't think of time
passing slow and turning back?

Reflections warp and blur
your face, your look, what it was,

passing slow and turning back,
you meant to say and wouldn't.

The surface shivers and wobbles, molten,
as if what never happened might happen still

folded back on itself. Afloat, it seems
what happened never happened and happens still.

Fingering the Chords for *Blackberry Blossom*

Dragged by the leash down to the creek—
a river modeled in miniature, its source strip mall runoff,
its end in the end the Potomac, the bay, the Atlantic.

I let the dog sniff what he sniffs, reviewing
the creek's recent memories—deer, dogs, kids, foxes…
I'm more inclined toward other distractions—

the whether, how, how soon. There's science
for what happens next, chance rules just
in the short run. We keep on, our path

automatic underfoot, around the washed-out
roots of a poplar, past a broad holly,
and over a fallen maple. Blackberries

bloom in the dappled places, calling to mind
the fiddle tune and old friends who played it.
Then we're at the woods' edge and step out

into unmown open field. Martins wheel
across the high grass tips. The dog,
being dog, can't help but want to snatch them

like balls from the air. I, being human,
can't help but admire and fret.
This field is Memorial land. When the dead

have used up the landscaped grounds
beyond the rise, management will mow,
fertilize, and spray so more bodies can be buried.

By then the dog and I won't care.

Abstraction

The damp tastes of decay, the blackstrap muck
        underfoot; molds and mushrooms and lichens
pale, no longer burning lime or acid orange.
        A drop of mist condensed
on every leaf tip, every bared arm hair.

        In a cloud come to earth
what's visible and what's not shifts,
        roots and vines and branches, and I
get lost, (in a good way)
        ten minutes from home; blurred,

the once-green, fine-cut ferns
        abstract to gray as-if-gestural brushwork,
redwing blackbird cries
        leave ionized tracks on the mind.
Everything tangent, contingent, porous, osmosing—

        the membranes between blood and air,
creek, moss, leaf, and mud placental.
        There's no such thing as discreteness,
separate forms among separate others.
        And then in no time sun

and light winds undo the mist,
        and lives, things—the edges of things—
appear as from nowhere. Imagined
        space contracts, a path to open marsh
clears, pussy willow and bramble untangle.

        From two or three ecotones off, low ocean
white noise restarts. Voices carry
        inland from the pier,
where every summer day
        kids drop their homemade traps

and haul them up amazed, shouting
        the same wild shout every time,
as up from the murky half-salt creek
        spider crabs, calicoes, and blues emerge,
a mess of tumbled-up, overlapped lives.

Happy Hour

As the skin of a flounder darkens

In shadow the mind also adjusts

Gravity is suspended in a gathering wave

One can for whole moments float

Unencumbered camouflaged

In ocean as ocean salt in salt

Crossing the cloud low overhead

A prop plane drags HAPPY HOUR 4-6!

Happiness in prospect already

In retrospect submerged in greens

The waking mind dissolves

A flounder the color of sand rests in sand

On Purpose to See

the migration, I walked the sumac and pine scruff dunes,

lay back in the sand, and as in a dream, overhead
monarchs the unlikely color of opium poppies, paper
lanterns, candy wrappers, wafted and lapsed in desultory flight.

Winds off the bay blustered and dropped, shut and flared
their wings as they lofted by twos and threes—
the migration nearly over. Once I saw seven together,

no dizzy spectacular, this straggler migration.
And the last salt asters, goldenrod, fleabane gone by,
wax myrtles shriveled to skin and seed. What if I *were*

a butterfly dreaming? When I closed my eyes
I listened: the surf's slow pulse
Mount, fall, rush, retract. A chickadee sang.

A chickadee sang in a stunted tree.

Barefoot, skirting the bay's shifting edge, I—
who could be happier?— picked up at random
smooth stones, white and green on my tongue.

Sandpipers skittered, nervous, wasting their strength
flying from me. I'll tell you what I didn't see:
a porpoise skull, a live conch, anything

to write home about. But—it's hardly worth
mentioning—there at the tideline broken-off
wings were caught in the seaweed-etc. tangle.

I tossed a few back to the wind and they twirled,
gold, tipped sideways like wings, and each one
separately, sailed a few seconds, not

really flying before they fell back.

Acknowledgments

I would like to gratefully acknowledge the editors of these literary journals in which the poems first appeared, often in slightly different form and/or under another title:

Association of Franciscan Colleges and Universities Journal: "Landscape with Jeffers and the Connecticut River," "Landscape with Bloodroot"
The Cincinnati Review: "The Laws of Succession"
december: "Almost," "Involution," "Abstraction"
Field: "On Earth As It Is," "The Thinking Eye"
Kaimana: "Drawn from Memory," "Local History"
The Missouri Review: "At the Chernobyl Power Plant Eco-Reserve," "Landscape with Translucent Moon," "The Understory," "Landscape with Peregrine Falcon and Hart Crane," "Fingering the Chords for *Blackberry Blossom*'"
New Madrid: "Reading By Riverlight"
Ruminate: "Fossil Record"
Shenandoah: "In the Hands of the Builder"
Sou'wester: "A Carolina Wren Sings on the Porch Rail," "The Seven Stars of the Little Dipper"
Subtropics: "Landscape of One Hundred Words"
Switchback: "The Understory"
Terrain: "Local History" (a reprint), "Still, Again: Thirty Years After the Assault"
U-City Review: "Landscape at 3rd Ave. and 1984"
Witness: "Landscape with Mud Turtle," "Landscape with Goat's Eye"

Thanks too to *Poetry Daily,* which reprinted "Landscape with Mud Turtle" and "Landscape with Translucent Moon" and to Melissa Tuckey, the editor of *Ghost Fishing: An Eco-Justice Poetry Anthology,* which reprinted "At the Chernobyl Power Plant Eco-Reserve" and "Landscape with Translucent Moon."

And to the Vermont Studio Center, The Brown Foundation's Dora Maar House, and The Porches.

I am even more grateful for the close and generous attention of my readers, especially the Sunday Poetry Group, Allison Funk, Jeff Hamilton, and most of all, my favorite poet, Eric Pankey.

"Landscape at 3rd Ave and 1984" is dedicated to Bob Crum and Jan Weissmiller.

"On Earth As It Is" is for John Slack, "The Understory" is for Marvin Bell, and "Fingering the Chords for *Blackberry Blossom*" is for Mike.

About the Author

Jennifer Atkinson is the author of five collections of poetry—*The Dogwood Tree, The Drowned City, Drift Ice, Canticle of the Night Path* (New Measure Poetry Prize), and *The Thinking Eye.* Individual poems have appeared in various journals including *Field, Image, Witness, New American Writing*, and *The Missouri Review.* She teaches in the English Department and the MFA and BFA programs at George Mason University in Virginia.

Phototgraph of the author by Eric Pankey. Used by permission.

Free Verse Editions

Edited by Jon Thompson

13 ways of happily by Emily Carr
Between the Twilight and the Sky by Jennie Neighbors
Blood Orbits by Ger Killeen
The Bodies by Chris Sindt
The Book of Isaac by Aidan Semmens
Canticle of the Night Path by Jennifer Atkinson
Child in the Road by Cindy Savett
Condominium of the Flesh by Valerio Magrelli, trans. by Clarissa Botsford
Contrapuntal by Christopher Kondrich
Country Album by James Capozzi
The Curiosities by Brittany Perham
Current by Lisa Fishman
Dismantling the Angel by Eric Pankey
Divination Machine by F. Daniel Rzicznek
Erros by Morgan Lucas Schuldt
The Forever Notes by Ethel Rackin
The Flying House by Dawn-Michelle Baude
Instances: Selected Poems by Jeongrye Choi, translated by Brenda Hillman, Wayne de Fremery, & Jeongrye Choi
The Magnetic Brackets by Jesús Losada, translated by Michael Smith & Luis Ingelmo
A Map of Faring by Peter Riley
No Shape Bends the River So Long by Monica Berlin & Beth Marzoni
Pilgrimly by Siobhán Scarry
Physis by Nicolas Pesque, translated by Cole Swensen
Poems from above the Hill & Selected Work by Ashur Etwebi, translated by Brenda Hillman & Diallah Haidar
The Prison Poems by Miguel Hernández, translated by Michael Smith
Puppet Wardrobe by Daniel Tiffany
Quarry by Carolyn Guinzio
remanence by Boyer Rickel
Signs Following by Ger Killeen
Split the Crow by Sarah Sousa
Spine by Carolyn Guinzio
Spool by Matthew Cooperman
Summoned by Guillevic, translated by Monique Chefdor & Stella Harvey
Sunshine Wound by L. S. Klatt

These Beautiful Limits by Thomas Lisk
The Thinking Eye by Jennifer Atkinson
An Unchanging Blue: Selected Poems 1962–1975 by Rolf Dieter Brinkmann, translated by Mark Terrill
Under the Quick by Molly Bendall
Verge by Morgan Lucas Schuldt
The Wash by Adam Clay
We'll See by George Godeau, translated by Kathleen McGookey
What Stillness Illuminated by Yermiyahu Ahron Taub
Winter Journey [Viaggio d'inverno] by Attilio Bertolucci, translated by Nicholas Benson
Wonder Rooms by Allison Funk

www.ingramcontent.com/pod-product-compliance
Ingram Content Group UK Ltd.
Pitfield, Milton Keynes, MK11 3LW, UK
UKHW041644190726
13854UKWH00006B/2681